GRACES
for Children

William Collins Sons & Co Ltd
London · Glasgow · Sydney · Auckland
Toronto · Johannesburg

First published 1989
© text Elizabeth Laird 1989
© illustrations William Collins Sons & Co Ltd 1989

ISBN 0 00 195435-0

Printed and bound in Belgium by
Proost International Book Production

GRACES
for Children

Elizabeth Laird
pictures by Mary Cooper

COLLINS

Breakfast time

Morning is here,
The night is done.
Breakfast is ready,
The day has begun.
Give us, Lord,
Your joy today,
In all we do
At work and play.

For happy mealtimes

Teach us, O Lord,
to cook our food lovingly,
to share it joyfully,
to eat it gratefully,
and to clear it up willingly.

A grace for every day

Lord, you know what we need
even before we ask you,
and you give us each day
our daily bread.
Help us to eat it
with grateful hearts.

Remembering others

While we eat, others are hungry.
May we never be greedy for more.
While we are warm, others are cold.
May we always remember them.

A grace for a picnic

Heavenly Father, you feed the birds,
and plant the blackberries in the
hedgerow.
We thank you for the flowers and the
birdsong, and for delicious food in the
open air.

When friends come

Lord Jesus, friend of children,
bless our friends today
and bless the food we share with them.

A baby's grace

Thank you God for Mummy.*
Thank you for my tea.
God bless the food we eat.
God bless Mummy and me.

*or Daddy, Granny etc.

A birthday grace

Light a flame of love in our hearts,
Lord, as we light the candles on the
birthday cake.

A Christmas grace

We give thanks for our Christmas
dinner,
On this day of our Saviour's birth,
With glory to God in the highest,
And peace to men on earth.

A family grace

All good things come from you,
O Lord, our family and friends, our
health and strength, and this food we
eat together.

A grace for all seasons

Oh God, you send the summer's sun,
The autumn wind, the winter snow.
You bring the gentle springtime rain,
That makes the wheat and barley grow.
It's by your hand that we are fed,
And so we thank you for our bread.

Thanks for home-made things

For home-made bread
and cakes and jam
and home grown fruit
from our apple tree,
we thank you, Lord.

In the evening

Evening is here,
gone is the sun.
Our supper's ready,
our work is done.
Give us Lord
your peace tonight.
In the darkness
give us light.